BOHDAN IHOR ANTONYCH

Night Music

Selected Poems

Translated from the Ukrainian by Stephen Komarnyckyj

KLP
Kalyna Language Press Limited

First published in the UK in 2016 by Kalyna Language Press Limited
Copyright - Kalyna Language Press 2016 All rights reserved. No part of this publication may be reproduced or transmitted in any form or by any means, electronic or mechanical, including photocopy, recording or otherwise without prior permission in writing from the publisher.

Acknowledgements

Cover Design by Kalyna Language Press
Poems in this book have previously been published in Almost Island, Modern Poetry in Translation, and on the And Other Stories website, with the support of the Jan Michalski Foundation and as part of a cooperation with the European Society of Authors.

ISBN: 978-0-9931972-7-7

This book has been selected to receive financial assistance from English PEN's "PEN Translates!" programme, supported by Arts Council England. English PEN exists to promote literature and our understanding of it, to uphold writers' freedoms around the world, to campaign against the persecution and imprisonment of writers for stating their views, and to promote the friendly co-operation of writers and the free exchange of ideas. www.englishpen.org

This book has been selected to receive financial assistance from English PEN's Writers in Translation programme supported by Bloomberg and Arts Council England. English PEN exists to promote literature and its understanding, uphold writers' freedoms around the world, campaign against the persecution and imprisonment of writers for stating their views, and promote the friendly co-operation of writers and free exchange of ideas.

Each year, a dedicated committee of professionals selects books that are translated into English from a wide variety of foreign languages. We award grants to UK publishers to help translate, promote, market and champion these titles. Our aim is to celebrate books of outstanding literary quality, which have a clear link to the PEN charter and promote free speech and intercultural understanding.

In 2011, Writers in Translation's outstanding work and contribution to diversity in the UK literary scene was recognised by Arts Council England. English PEN was awarded a threefold increase in funding to develop its support for world writing in translation.
www.englishpen.org

Bohdan Ihor Antonych

Night Music

Selected poems

Contents

Introduction   11
Bibliography and Glossary   17

Poems

Duet   19
Self Portrait   20
Bitter Wine   21
Conversation with a Leaf   22
Forest   23
Of Bulls and Beeches   24
To My Song   25
Crazy Fish   26
Spring   27
The Wind at Dawn   29
Of Merchants and Girls   30
Meeting   31
The Green Thoughts of One Fox   32
(jottings from Antonych's notebook)
Landscape Through a Window   33
Always   34
Spring Night   35
Chalices   36
Spindle   37
Primal Summer   38
Maples   40
Eight Ecstatic Verses   41
Village   43
Zelman   44
The Green Gospel   45
A Song on the Indestructibility of Matter   46
Serpent   47

Night	48
The Blackthorn's Complaint	49
Koliada	50
Square of Angels	51
The Gold Sea	52
Above the Water	53
Idyll	54
The Carp	55
Roses	56
Apocalypse	57
Polar	58
Storm	59
Alders	60
A Miracle	61
Prophetic Oak	62
Fatherland	63
A Double Concert	64
Extract	65
Crossing	66
Forgotten Soil	67
A Word to the War Dead	68
Invitation	69
Life According to the Greek Bios	70
To the Being from the Green Star	71
An Epic Evening	72
The First Chapter of the Bible	73
Nuptial	74
The Wedding Night	75
Hops	76
Two Hearts	77
Hooves	78
Periwinkle Sincerity	79
A Little Hymn	80
Market	81

Cuckoo	82
The Home Beyond the Stars	83
Science	85
To the Depths	86
Daily Bread	87
The Sign of the Oak	88
Orchard	89
Tavern Enchantments	90
Haymaking	91
A Fig of a Verse	92
The Guelder Rose	93
Skiers	94
Winter	96
Sunset	97
Antonych Grows	98
Cherries	99
Myth	100
The Emissaries of Night	101
The Wind of Centuries	103
Village	104
Roofs	105
Circle	106
Country of Annunciation	107
Two Chapters from the Liturgy of Love	108
To a Proud Plant, that is, to Myself	109
Rotation	110
Of Cities and Muses	112
War Drum	114
Ballad of the Alleyway	116
The Ballad of Azure Death	118
Doomsday Cometh	119
A Concert from Mercury	120
Dead Cars	121
The Last Trumpet	122

A Poem about the Breezes	123
Night	126
Green Faith	127
Musica Noctis: Night Music	128
Amen	129
De Morte IV	130
Idolatrous Nights	131
In Conclusion	133

Introduction

1 Prelude

I first stumbled across Antonych in a musty edition of his work I purchased in 1993, during my first trip to Ukraine. The book was an impulse buy, partly because I was sickened by what I encountered in my ancestral homeland. Hyperinflation had transformed my auntie into a 'millionaire' and the interim kupony currency seemed to breed zeroes, like bacteria in a petri dish. A woman, the sickly yellow colour of ill health, fainted at a bus stop. Stalagmites of urine crystallised in the latrines of Kyiv station. I was in a country that was being born but, if there was a birth, there was a death also. When I opened the book it was like peering into a portal with a view onto another world. The cover may have been grey but Antonych wrote in hologrammatic ink. He evoked a Ukraine as fecund and pungent as a rain forest, where pagan gods haunted the shadows. His poetry has only rarely appeared in English. He is, for most Anglophone readers, an unknown quantity, as obscure as the Carpathian mountains glimpsed through the mist. Who was Antonych? Where was he from? And why is this translation necessary?

2 The Pagan

There are some old photographs, which seem to preserve the subject in the amber light of a previous decade. Bohdan Ihor Antonych stares back at us from the thirties, sometimes with owlish spectacles, looking preternaturally boyish. He grew up in the Lemky area of Ukraine, which was then part of Poland, and was the son of a rural priest. The Lemky (Ukrainian: "Лемки") were an ancient Ukrainian mountain tribe who lived a life that had remained unchanged for centuries. Their farmsteads and villages were shadowed by Carpathian mountain peaks like mute, indifferent gods. Their Ukrainian was rich with dialect words and their lives were governed by the rhythms of the seasons. The old, pagan deities lingered among the pine forests and haunted a superficially Christianised world. Antonych proudly declared himself a pagan and his poetry is redolent of the peasant's affinity with nature. Yet he was, like John Clare, another superficially peasant poet, a deeply read and profoundly skilful writer. In his poetry, the boundaries between the narrator, the natural world and the music of the poems become blurred within an ecstatic pagan celebration of life. His boyish face reflects his almost perpetual sense of rapture, not only with nature, but with the human world. He can exalt in the sound of jazz from behind a wall in an alleyway, a heap of rusted cars, and a cloud shadow sailing over the pasture. This seemingly effortless febrile absorption in life masks his dedication to his craft. Antonych was only 27 when he died but lived several lives in one lifetime, producing six collections of poetry, reams of prose, an opera libretto and an unfinished novel, as well as editing a couple of journals.

Although he would have been surrounded by people speaking the Lemky dialect in his childhood, he attended a Ukrainian language grammar school and, between 1928 and 1933, L'viv University. He wrote in literary Ukrainian, but his work was sprinkled with dialect terms and fevered energetic imagery. Moss warms "like cat fur", and the nocturnal forest becomes an orchestra playing music that manifests itself as light. He uses many verse forms, ranging from sonnets comprising two quatrains and two tercets, to free verse, and numerous improvised stanza forms.

Antonych's death deprived Europe of one of the greatest talents of his generation. His work, with its mystic overtones, was ignored by the soviets. Starting from the mid-

1960s, interest in his writing has revived in the Ukrainian diaspora, but he remains relatively unknown. His poetry, with its elemental power, is a worthy introduction to a great and neglected national literature.

3 The impossible country

Antonych and Ukrainian language literature remain curiously invisible in the Anglophone world. I could pick up English university text books in the seventies and see Ukrainian described as a dialect and its literature as "minor". The West was blind to the reality of intra-European colonisation. The views of Ukraine's colonising power, Russia, were treated as if they had the scientific validity of Boyle's law. What I might call the Russian paradigm of a primitive Ukrainian peasantry being civilised by its more advanced neighbour prevailed. This is a gross untruth, yet it means that Ukrainian is reflexively treated as inferior.

However, Ukrainian literature has distinct qualities that renders it neither better nor worse than Russian, but merely different. Taras Shevchenko (1814-1861) may have been the only major nineteenth century European poet ever to have been owned by another human being. Tsar Nicholas I personally wrote on the order condemning him to exile that Shevchenko was "forbidden to write or to paint" (Plokhy 49). He and many other Ukrainian authors represent, better than their Russian counterparts, the voice of the empire's oppressed masses. In his work the often mute or comic peasantry of Gogol (or Hohol in its original Ukrainian form) and Chekhov acquires a tender humanity. The latter authors grew up speaking Ukrainian. However, the empire's linguistic policy, its effective banning of a language, led to them writing in Russian, infusing that language with a quirky Ukrainian lyricism and grotesquerie. Even today there are a small and diminishing number of writers who translate their text internally into Russian. The very act of writing in Ukrainian was, therefore, an act of rebellion against imperial hegemony. Then, as now, the language's subversive status resulted in a fecund experimentalism. Rory Finnin of Cambridge University notes that Ukrainian is therefore a literature of "rebels and risk takers" (Finnin).

The Empire, of course, always strikes back and, indeed, usually delivers the first blow. The long standing animosity towards Ukrainian culture emanating from Russia was summarised in a Chatham House paper of 2012:

Taras Shevchenko's legacy, Ukrainian language, and the Ukrainian 'national idea' of the last two centuries ... appear to be meaningless, second-rate or blasphemous to a large number of Russians. Generations of Russian intellectuals have turned belittling of the Ukrainian language and culture into a part of the Russian belief system, alongside anti-Tatar and anti-Muslim stereotypes. But, whereas the latter are built around national differences, what makes Ukraine stand out in this list is a dismissive attitude to any assertion that national differences exist.

(Bogomolyov and Lytvynenko, 2012)

However, Antonych, of course, lived and died in a west Ukraine that was under Polish control. During this period, the Polish State actively pursued the assimilation of Ukrainians via a programme of Polonisation. Polish language was imposed upon Ukrainians and they were required to formally identify as Poles in order to access certain occupations. Ukrainians, of course, are both perpetrators and victims within the history of their colonisation by other peoples. However, the cultural repression they experienced explains why their literature was marginalised internationally. Poland and Ukraine are embarking on a difficult process of reconciliation. Russia remains opposed to the very existence of Ukraine and still focuses on damaging the country's image internationally.

4 Antonych the poet

Antonych's work, and that of many other Ukrainian poets, survives because of that unique spirit which we have in part described, a fusion of literary talent and a pagan, rebellious spirit. I have noted that the very act of writing in Ukrainian was political. Antonych entered an ecstatic state to write his poetry. He is able to convey transcendence through his absolute commitment to his craft. He is also the representative of a pagan culture that survived, relatively unchanged, from the dark ages. He combines the visionary qualities of Blake or Clare with Shelley's craftsmanship and David Gascoyne's manic inventiveness. However, his brief life meant that his work represents only a fraction of his potential.

5 Duet

Why did I translate this book? There are other translations of Antonych which faithfully duplicate his verse forms and the structure of his collections in English. Yet his poetry has been cited twice, in 2013 and 2015, in the Finnegan's List produced by the European Society of Authors. The list, which is drafted by prominent European authors, consists of work that is not sufficiently represented in translation.

Antonych has never been translated by a poet whose primary concern was to create a book of poetry in English and build him a reputation among readers, rather than linguists. This book is aimed at the reader of poetry who will, perhaps, have an image of Ukraine shaped by Russian soft power. My aim has not been to duplicate every one of his devices in

English. All Antonych's poems are finely wrought, he loads "every seam with ore". Yet, if we reflected all these devices in English, we would murder the poem in the target language. As Jeremy Reed says:

poets are too often worked dead by translation. The substitution of one language for another, the attempt to match, word for word, the creative potential of the original, which is animated by virtue of the imagination charging the language, is the perfect means to making a poet redundant in a foreign language
(Montale 9)

If we are to render Antonych's poetry effectively into English, we must reckon with the traditions of both languages. The poems in this collection are what Ukrainians might term a perespiv, a song over a song, and attempt to provide him with an English voice. I have structured the book so that it has the emotional logic of a collection of English poetry. The reader will perceive echoes of Dylan Thomas, W.B. Yeats, John Keats, and Percy Bysshe Shelley in these poems. Antonych's poetry is both richly Ukrainian and yet it "has no nation but the imagination" (Walcott). His work belongs to that great literature which speaks to the one abiding collective, humanity.

Bibliography

Bogomolyov, Alexander and Lytvynenko Oleksandr, January 2012: A Ghost in the Mirror: Russian Soft Power in Ukraine Briefing Paper
http://www.chathamhouse.org/publications/papers/view/181667
(Accessed 19 August 2016)

Finnin, Rory 31 October 2012: The Rebels and Risk Takers of Ukrainian Literature
http://www.huffingtonpost.co.uk/dr-rory-finnin/rebels-and-risktakers_b_2042844.html
(Accessed 19 August 2016)

Plokhy, Serhii: The Cossack Myth: History and Nationhood in the Age of Empires. Cambridge University Press 2012

Montale, Eugenio: The Coastguard's House. English versions by Jeremy Reed. Tarset, Bloodaxe 1990

Walcott, Derek: The Schooner Flight (Original Source: Poems 1965-1980 (Jonathan Cape, 1980))
http://www.poetryfoundation.org/poem/177932 (Accessed 15 April 2014)

Glossary

Horilka - the Ukrainian word for vodka
Horlitsi - the Ukrainian name for Gorlice
Kalyna- the Ukrainian name for the Guelder Rose, a plant with enormous significance to Ukrainians
Koliada - Christmas carolling
Lemky - a Ukrainian mountain tribe

Duet

We return slowly to the earth, our cradle.
Green tangles of vegetation bind us, two fettered chords.
The razor sharp axe of sun hews at a trunk,
The music of moss, tenderness of the breeze, the oak a proud
                                                                          idol.

In the wastage of days that bear us the body, warm and
                                                                          obedient
Grows with itself, two siblings, two flowers of fidelity.
The moss warms us like cat fur. You transform the stars into a
                                                                          murmur
And blood into music and greenery. The sky glows.

At the edge of day, in the ocean of heaven, the winds of the
                                                                      future sleep
And our devoted constellations wait under the frost,
While earth does not instruct them to arise. We abandon
                                                                           things,
To be borne, to grasp the stars in pure ecstasy.

The yearning of blood hurts. Eyebrows sharp as two arrows,
While above us a wall of melody echoes
The pinions of a breeze. Our fate pinned on the planets.
You burn with growth, thirsty as the earth. Become all music.

Self Portrait

The red maples and the maples silver,
Spring and the wind above them.
Beauty, boundless, raw and new,
How could I not get wasted on you?

I sold my life to the sun
For a hundred ducats of craziness,
I'm the enraptured pagan,
The poet drunk with spring.

Bitter Wine

My days are harsh and cold,
Songs redolent of wormwood,
Horizons drowned in the infinite
Depths of this dark spring.

Alluring words whispered
Into my ear, intoxicating poison,
That stills the heart's blizzard
At least for a moment.

Anaesthetic days I compose
This poisonous tribute to my times
In vain. I must drink the bitter wine
Of poetry myself, alone.

The unwise dream I call gladly,
Knowing it is false, a phantom:
I long to carve out the day's face
With the chisel of verse.

Conversation with a Leaf

The hand of autumn touches this pond,
A crane's call, "kru", falls on the waves,
The distance expands all around,
The clouds are imprinted with stars.

My hand dents a small leaf from the soil.
Oh, how it brims with winter's apparitions,
Its form yet holding a fragment of summer.
Small leaf, my withered friend.

The last pound of life has dispersed…
The wind played it away, a liar,
When you squabbled about happiness…

But do not grieve, having spring, know this
Craft is also often happiness,
Self-knowledge often found while you booze.

Forest

Study the forest's language
From the book of foxes and antelopes!
The moon enters the groves,
Writes elegies on tree stumps.

Streams rinse silence with silver,
Dew bathes the grass,
Let night scribble the simplest words
In the book of the forest.

Of Bulls and Beeches

Plants flow over forested terraces of soil,
Are a misty wall, green streams pulse
Above tree trunks. The sun's yellow flame
Is honey
Oozing through a holed barrel.
Tree bark blazes auburn,
Speckled with strawberries of sunshine.

Again the wind rolls night's wheel
From the forested foot hills,
From the periphery of stars,
Where the shadows of meadows pale.
A stream
Desiccated with ecstasy cries
The memory of ancient waters,

Earth threatens the malevolent stars
With the wrath of beeches.
Decayed stumps protrude
From the soil's maw. Day comes.
A star
Vainly beseeches blood,
And falls, pale with despair,

Empty words upon the breast
Of a dawn thicketed with mist.
The stumps sleep,
The soul within an extinguished fire
And beech locks horns with beech
In the cave of night
Until the sun's skirt all crimson

Dabs the blood from them.

To My Song

The world rotates, vernal and green,
The ash tree sings, my heart sings also,
Song inspired by swirl of spindle,
Spindle where my words turn silver.

Ash tree, sun splendoured, drunken,
Ring inspired on my heart trembling,
Oh, fly and swirl my drunken one
Of three and twenty years, my song!

Crazy Fish

For Poets

The water sprays, spurts, burbles and babbles,
Playing melodies on a flute of stone,
White foam of the multi-maned waves harry
Fish faces from dark depths bloom, and one

Vaults over the waves, beating
The sun to a wheel with its flight,
Falls back. Then the waves have another tone,
Solitary and taciturn, though young.

The silver fibres of water
Are where you dream
Looking up like a crazy fish,
Which once glimpsed the sun.

Spring

Spring, and chirpy chimney sweeps
Sway like goldfinches on rooftops in green mist.
The girl who loves a policeman sings
In the square where her car was stolen,
The conductor of a choir of curvaceous cars
Holds in his gloves, so white,
A piece of sun.

Green balloons,
Bouquets of the first childhood dreams,
Sway in the fist
Of a boy
Who weeps for them quietly.

The children, afraid of the black chimney sweeps,
Grip their buttons hard,
Day shakes green shadows in the heart,
They bow to it, in the peony's
Crimson armouries.

Are they sparks from lush green flowers
Or rose foam, scuffed up by a foot?
No, butterflies float light as dust in a line
Through pooling sunlight, wing bathing,
Till gold soot covers everything.
Sparks from a rainbow they light
Spring's green basket.

You can buy the speckled balloon for ten farthings,
A dream of youth, daring and vivid,
Buoyant as the flight of goldfinches.

The girl with an armful of wet roses,
Sings like the cuckoo, long and with yearning,
Above the carousel of city square
His truncheon sways blue silver.

The Wind at Dawn

Wind, soaring and powerful that bears
Stars, leaves and swallows, intoxicates
The heart. Oh to fly into
Green April, blue distances of song.

Day rises, an antelope by the river.
Night sails away
And the wind soars
In clashing sabres.

Of Merchants and Girls

An old tale tells
Of merchants and girls,
A glass levitates in a hand,
Desire and drink thicken the blood.

Ducats ring on the table, the moon
Is the most intoxicating chalice.
Dusk bows to the soil,
And the river's silver stencil.

Meeting

The boy grows like a raspberry bush,
Horseshoes ring on pathways,
Swallows inscribe in the bird book
The advent of day.

Yoking the sun to a calf
I go to meet the spring,
In resurrected snow
April's young days sing.

The Green Thoughts of One Fox
(jottings from Antonych's notebook)

Sea roars with the voice of a shell, jugs its cold drink,
Earth, mammoth shaggy with green grass solar heat...
Forests soar...
He crushed underfoot the sun,
Now it rests on him like a tombstone.

In my skull two serpents twine in their nuptial bed
Is it so? So, will we not live forever, beloved?
Where does the boundary of life pass to the ashes of death?

Look into the lips, how they cry
Into the laughing eyes of fire,
Faces carved into memory
To pour them into song.

The souls of trees,
Yearning to fly to the moon
But the wind does not gather them.

Night casts its horseshoe of stars into the palms of story
                                        where it's lost.

Strange letters in the sylvan alphabet.
For example, the acorn means "u"
In the woodpeckers' dialect the knocking
On a tree trunk transmits this phoneme.

Landscape Through a Window

Look: roar of sunny day,
Boiling greenery,
A vessel where the pink
Foam of roses simpers

And rain spatters the windows
With cinnabar.

Horizons evaporate,
Are dust, waves of smoke
From dawn's salvoes.
You lift your eyes from a book,

Life is briefly a dream
Imagination colours in,
Thought escapes on tiptoe
A moth against the window.

Always

Men in grey coats drown in the alley's indigo,
Shadows smear over the ladies like torn pictures.
Gold tea in a glass. You yearn
To lean through the window frame,
Into that harsh overwhelming blueness,
And drink the cold,
Looking at that morose star
In the firmament.
Night's azure snow
Washes over the melancholy poppies,
Coating the arched sky with blue.
The chauffeur jolts in his sleeping limousine.
The crooked street lamp is a broken flower, is ashes,
Its viscous green light decanted
From the jug of night
Into the gliding shadows of dusk.
The crooked and dark steps, the tattered coat, the smile drops, lost,
And the moon
Is a white bird, vicious and exalted,
The silk bullet of dreaming cutthroats,
Hidden in shadows
That, like the strings of a violin perhaps,
Once touched your heart.
Touched and kissed it proudly and tenderly
As eyelids touch soundlessly over closed eyes,
Tender as the farewell
To a last sister.
Men in grey coats pull stars out of their pockets
And pay ladies for love, just for five minutes,
Hunched shoulders dressed in the sky's blue pelt
And the chauffeur in his sleeping limousine jolts.

Spring Night

Night of nasturtiums
And lilies of the valley,
Radio music floats through the orchard,
I wait for you
As night burns,
Eve, my distant star.

The nocturne's tenor,
Its Caruso, is the moon
Calling us into the blackness of a radio
Too small to hold our thoughts
Or love
Secret and eternal.

Its light is too scant
For our hearts and the earth
And exaltation are too small for us,
Though the morning
Blusters in
Sweeping night from roads with spring.

Chalices

Green ash tree, sickle and a horse,
The boy presses against the glass,
In its chalice, silver and crimson,
All of spring is decanted.

How he yearns,
For the key to those vernal gates,
When the sun springs and a startled
Pony from grass levitates.

Spindle

Day, a piercing arrow, translucent and cold
As elusive beauty.
You draw a circle broad with song,
Blue-silver sky, fragrant with morning.

The soul is a violin string,
The snow laughs and I laugh also,
A young boy's twirl
Around the sun's red spindle.

Primal Summer

1

We bathe in the pine sea
In the murmur of pines, their song,
Above us a starless sky,
A roof of slender tree crowns
Respiring deeply.
Trunks glide away.

You feel beneath your footstep
Things grow green and fragrant.

Here we desire nothing more,
Sleep swaddled in moss,
In nature's primal dusk,
Ancient depths where we are fallen.

Let the dense sap seethe
In our body, as in the pines,
Let there be languid green in our veins,
Let the flame fade to azure.

2

We grow in the earth like the pines,
The banners of the forest flapping,
Plant juice, green blood,
Flows in our lethargic veins,
Legs thrust roots into clay,
Pine needles from palms sprout,
Bees settle on our eyes, sip
Honey from them as flowers.

Blood is no more, is heavy oil
That splashes in our hardening centre,
Like a raspberry, dream ripens
Sweet, ardent and drunken.

You grow by the edge of the road,
A crimson bush amidst silence,
Broken only by an antelope,
A slender legged loner seeking
A timid roe.

Maples

Two solitary maples lean
Reading the alphabet of spring,
  Again I pray to the green earth,
  Myself green as grass.

The learned fox, sprouting moss
Composes poetry for the maples.
  Day sings and maples sing also,
  Loosing a solar arrow.

Eight Ecstatic Verses

The green seed of flax whispers in my temples,
Its warm, greasy dust twists among oils,
As always in the curves of lime trees, the curse explodes,
Of a green, angry and restless soul.

The worms do not submit to the untamed stream of life
Where woodpeckers strike sparks from the trees
And, paying the day with its coined stars, the evening
Buys the sun that adorns his crimson moss.

A red sash of light is draped over the lime trees,
That sift rays onto the dozing family,
The strings of leaf are silenced by the abrupt touches
Of the breeze that disrupts the quietness gently.

The girls open their bodies, faintly smelling
Of flax oil, to their lovers, as flowers,
And the sun explodes with a demented ring
When it strikes the dense cymbal of clouds drunkenly.

Everything falls quietly into an insane hymn
That oozes, like a poppy cake, with grease,
And life is an untrammelled electric stream
In the roots of bodies, the veins of limes, mesh of trees.

Look! This is the world burning, a primal storm,
Where the plants pray and each colour goes loco,
Where roots exhale a subterranean breeze and the lime
They respire through is a clarinet picking up the lead solo.

The trees, the chimneys of the earth, exhale
In a green, gold, purpled fume,
Above the gold sea spray of straw, in the farewell
Dust of the sun and the birds that depart with them.

The sunrise, summer and lime trees dreaming
The perpetual mutability of dusk and dawn,
I praise the vigorous labour of oil, the burning,
Of souls, the body's ecstasy and lovers' intoxication.

Village

The cows pray to a sun
Petalled with fire,
The poplar is ever slenderer,
A tree shape shifting to a bird.

The moon unyoked from a cart,
Sky broad, blue as hemp flowers…
Endless distance respires,
The forest combs shreds of mist.

Sycamore leaves drift from mountains,
Wool cloud, cockerel and cradle.
Day flows down the hill
Fresh milk into a bowl.

Zelman

The endless world rotates
Greenery on earth and heaven,
The comb of sun plaits
Into the hair of maidens.

Day green and cruciform,
Happy ponies play fighting,
It's hard to put into song
Just what gives the soul wings.

Zelman and his white cart roll
Morning rings with troparias,
Oh, nuptial vine, please tell
Of my heart's drunkenness.

The Green Gospel

Spring, a carousel
On which white horses swirl,
Mountain village amidst cherry orchards;
The moon a red tulip.

A Slavic chest
On the ash table
Holds the sun inside.
Worship only the soil,

Where its radiance echoed.

A Song on the Indestructibility of Matter

Gathered into the thickets and wind swathed,
Sky covered and swaddled in song, I lie,
A wise fox beneath the flower of bracken,
I ripen, grow cold and harden to white stone.

A vegetable stream rears to a flood of green, to
Ceaseless cacophony of hours, comets and leaves
Decant flood into me, crush me with pale sun
So my body becomes coal and my songs will be ash.

Shunt of a thousand centuries laval
Where we, as nameless palm trees, sprout,
A black flower will bloom on our bodies' coal,
A miner's pickaxe will chime in my heart.

Serpent

Serpent supple as a plant and bushy,
Serpent coiled and slippery,
A wet chequered stick singing
In a boy's hands.

Serpent crested with rose petals,
Serpent crawling from stone under bush,
Words undulant and plantish,
That rain happily spatters.

Like the ferns before us
You are primeval too,
You are a plant, a stone also,
The serpent again, twisting you.

Night

The open book, a lamp, moths roaming
Rusted thoughts lay on the heart.
Shadows knit nooses on the wall,
In marvellous, baffling coils.

The squat teapot sits, a black cat,
My watch buzzes, a honey bee,
How sweet the alluring secret,
The word chiselled from stone.

Tin plated sky and leaden moon,
Night powdering into soot.
Is there anywhere at all
To achieve the impossible?

The Blackthorn's Complaint

Silence. Birds disturb the leaves no more,
The dark is empty as death's glance.
A cold light pierces the forest's recesses,
An eye looks unflinchingly at life's depths.

Droplets of blood from the night's wound,
Guelder rose berries redden amidst leaves.
Antelope, my brother, we are both made of clay
But you understand life better than me!

All we know for certain - there are more stars
Than poppy seeds and life loops like a bird's flight.
How every night the blackthorn complains
That it must pierce Christ's brow with its thorns.

Koliada

God was born on a sleigh
In Duklo, a Lemky town,
The Lemky came in their hats,
Bearing the round moon.

Night, and blizzards swirling
Around the rooftop.
Mary's palm clasps
The moon's gold walnut.

Square of Angels

The marble tenor on the theatre square
Has sung that gold star for two centuries,
Now night commands darkness to spin
Breath into a delicate yarn.

The factory girls go home and dream
That ardent tenors caress them,
While their throats are awash with song,
But feel only a ginger cat's nuzzling.

The lion sleeps by the arsenal.
At night he rises and roams the city,
Where song echoes from brothels,
The rain whispers freedom to jailed rebels.

The angels on the square are silent,
While red ink pours into the darkness.
The historian writes on his pedestal,
Dipping his quill deep in the inkwell.

The Gold Sea

The emissaries from the gold sea come in crimson rain,
Its stringed light sheers apart, the bee tribes madden,
Their wings playing interwoven chords, mist rears
And rain spurs its white horse into crimson berries.

The emissaries speak of stars in an unknown tongue.
Long ago mother sang of the underwater kingdom,
Where the sun sleeps, awash with light, and she sang
Of how the cart with wheels of seven stars came…

Sunset. Strings of rain frolic. Then silence tenses
And raspberries slowly turn ashen. You dream,
As if returning to the cradle quilted with moss
In the forest's bed. The shadow of leaves flickers…

The star breathes through the reed of a flute
The night's brow blooms a sacred oak, pastures
Stampede. You lay in the pelt of night, yet warm in faith.
The wise circle of life is complete. Love, alone,

Is stronger than death.

Above the Water

Silver birches on the bank, tense strings.
The day draws the wind over them,
A violin bow, and the whisper
Falls into the waves, as seed lisps into a barn.
The river hugs the sound deep in its breast.

The waves bud with foam
Splashes squabble among.

I stood on the bank
Caressing a sticky birch trunk
And chucked my dreams, my verse,
Into the water's face.

Idyll

On the riverbank, a white flock of sheep,
The wind raking clouds, heaven's pale mane,
Mist thick, grey, as unharvested rye.
Curved cloud sits on peak like a swan.

Flat mound, gold fish plashing in a ditch,
Where reality ends and imagination
Is the world non *est certum*. Horace writes a poem
On his balcony in Tusculum,

Listening to a concert
On the impossible radio. Music.

The Carp

The carp sing, razoring the water.
The wind lifts roofs like the lids of chests.
The birch reads a sermon to the perch.
This is all unreal and implausible,
Don't believe it.

But what I saw this morning was real enough.
Where the river washes the roots of the forest,
The wind was an ardent lover, who undressed
The girls to bathe, to be baptised and kissed.

Roses

The time of roses has passed, sister
So long they waited for it to come,
Bright acres blessed by the sun
Measured with soil and water.

Although this light was too frail,
Too early, and the snow too stubborn,
The sun frugal and the greenery bare,
Day was rich with unexpunged magic.

Washing our hands in the blood of roses,
In the first cooing of doves, we depart
Far, far away among the beeches,
Star with star and heart with heart.

Apocalypse

So they drift like drowsy, gigantic lions, the silhouettes
Of those heavy stone prisons rooted in soil,
And at night the prisoners are visited by lovers and comets,
And the moon, a bronze spider crawls slowly on the wall.

When words are worn to dust, it is vain to confess to the stars,
The stars where, as on these walls, there are mould and worms,
Painted green with dankness,
But the moon washes the faces of prisoners with its chill blue lustre,

Faces that, like the round platter of a sheared trunk,
Have overnight sprouted a pelt of moss!
The unctuous subterranean river, a nightmarish herb,
Writhes with moist stars and serpents,

The valleys of the moon, dense with walnut forests,
Where for a hundred days and nights the bronze rain and lamenting gales come,
The water bearing stars washes away the prison walls.
Where stone no longer stands on stone and the mountains are levelled.

The builders of walls raise a new prison from their straw hats
Abrim with flowers.
Beneath the gallows bloom purple mandragoras.
The rope of hanged men brings the living happiness.

Polar

Sea hardens to a chalice of ice,
The moon's gold lip hangs,
Polar angels guide the water,
Some animal keens.

Here there is nothing human.
A whale splashes the stars.
A white bird hovers,
Awakening the waters,

The ice carapace flexes.

The souls of mammoths roam
The snows as darkness comes.

Storm

A storm comes. The alders
Nestle together,
And beseech the sky
For mercy.

Lightning.
Poppies blink,
A red flag brandished
Against the dark.

The wind, a clarinet, wails.
That midnight astronomer
The fox calls
Through a papilloma
Of thunder.

Beyond the storm freedom
Excavates the clouds,
And the word
Is lightning crucified.

Alders

Spring kindles incense among alders,
Mornings redolent of chill blue sky,
The power of growth speaks its green codex
For the carp and tench, soundlessly.

The girls come to the pond sheltered by trees,
To press the rumpled linen of the clouds,
The wind tugs branch and leaf,
Trying to tear the sun from alders.

The heart once more finds a word,
Slender, infatuated and drunken,
Among a bright raspberry-tinged sky, like birds
The alders flying.

A Miracle

Dawn. Stars emerge from mist,
Gold buttons from a coat.
Day opens to familial poppies,
Stipples bushes with nightingales.

Valleys sleep in scrolled silence,
Contemplative moss and a lichen
Of mist. A fecund melon
Lolls on daisy leaf at dawn.

The sun, a melon too, wind shunted
Over the bright valley's sieve
The pupils of flowers flash,
Trees yearn to blue perspectives.

The heart's unquiet longing
To apprehend the depths of all
Crackles with leaves aspiring
Hurt for the day's miracle.

Prophetic Oak

The snow, green in the nocturnal light,
Blue at dawn
The oak, a prophet, rears
Its lyre on the horizon.

The snow heaps ashes at sunset.
Flames bloom.
The wounds bleed out
Into a gold kingdom.

Only the oak breasts that wide sea,
Denting the snow carapace,
Its dolphin glide
Renews life's promise.

Fatherland

Yellow gladioli bloom in the wet meadows
As in my childhood days on coils of mist.
Swallows fly,
Swift as years passing.

Gold coagulates in roses,
Wet stars blur into dusk.
The light of your youth flares,
Though another decade
Weighs on your shoulders.

Listen. Your fatherland calls its son
With the simplest of words.
Stars and faces reflect off the water,
And ripple
In its singing tongue
And dark-eyed people.

A Double Concert

Music seeps from the radio,
Its light illuminates the flowers
Till they loom huge
And ghostly in the darkness.

A minute flora of sounds sprouts,
A sea of radio waves
Casts melody's boat about,
Flowers and light compose

An enchanted cave,
Beneath the concert of blossoms
Like a punishment for the crime
Of trespassing against beauty,

The courtyard is a dark basket,
A realm of garbage where flowers
And music alike perish.
Look into the pit of death.

Oh can you, maestro of radiance,
Endure your own art?
It is not only they
Who are punished by beauty.

Extract

I am afraid to put out the light,
For things may become worse yet
And night composed in iambics,
A knife that killed my heart.

No chance of sleep. Yodelling roosters,
The clock ticks watching the moon descend,
My dream, my troubled voice,
My tragic fatherland.

Crossing

Cloud against cloud, the clatter of boards
Deafening strike and sky crackle,
Tipped from a shovel,
As sand's whispered chime off metal.
Guelder rose bears rain,
Soup in a leaf's green spoon,
Drinks and drinks its stream, some long yearned for
                                                happiness,
Like a family of splashes and the dew's kiss
Opening the burning cluster of its berries.
How the red tendril cluster sways,
The rain tenses taut rope,
The liberated gale rages in its circle.
Thirst seizes black desiccated lips,
The torn off branch rotates in the vortex and bliss
Grasps our round faces.
Our palms are written in the rhythm of love and keys of
                                                music.
You are the frightened fallow deer I seek,
Not as in the Bible on a bed of roses,
No, drink this fruitful storm, its kiss,
Perhaps
The earth is too small even for adoration,
Even as our all is become the storm!
Oh the tempest comes with its plainsong,
Thunder and thunder, as serpents inter plaiting
Our kiss woven
As, unknowingly, you give of yourself all
So, no,
Do not pull your hand away from mine,
Snap the rose on its stem.

Forgotten Soil

The village is not lit by candles at night
For it is afraid to wake the moon,
Which, a yellow nameless flower,
Blooms in the orchard, washed with rain.

Water oozes densely from levees
Where the horizons poise in flight
And, nested in the storm, side by side
Lay animals, people and comets.

The forgotten soil lies beneath the rain
Beneath the leaden, auburn sky,
Its song, a stone on the heart,
But all must sing it.

A Word to the War Dead

It's true that rain can wash blood from stone,
A crimson scarf can dab the moon clean,
But your names, redder than the deepest rose,
Burn in memory on plaques unerasable.

You strived passionately, dreamed and lived,
Loved in harsh times as ardently as we
In easy ones. Your eyes shone with eternity
When the bullet lodged its star in your heart.

Invitation

Day burns on the coal of night,
Evening rinses ashes from the grass,
Fear drills into your heart,
Moon scatters the shadows of the lost.

Lonely friend, like a sash in the night,
You are shrouded in the world's conundrum,
So come with me on this spring evening
And raise a glass of horilka to the moon.

Life According to the Greek Bios

Oats, butterflies and the oaths of lovers
Spring drunkenly, bends the spindles of May grass,
Foxes, martens and maidens in the morning,
Go to wash their eyes in creeks among wild reeds.

The sun's clock ticks away the hours with blooms,
Poppies close, confused in the evening,
Though beneath sky, boundless, unreachable,
Grow and spawn animals, plants, people.

To the Being from the Green Star

The laws of the 'bios' are alike for all
Birth, suffering and death.
What will remain of me: the ashes of my words.
What will remain of us: grass sprouts from bone.

Foxes, swallows, lions and people,
But worms and leaves of the green star
Surrendering to the immutable laws of matter
As the sky above us, blue and silver.

I understand you, animals and plants,
I feel how the comets murmur and the grass grows,
For Antonych too is a beast
With a pelt like yours, and morose.

An Epic Evening

The coppery leaved beeches, a banner
The sun rotates a platter of fire,
The meadow where suntanned boys murmur
Like bees, and dust explodes off rust-coloured brickwork.

The cows sway on the surf of grass, its green smoke,
They graze, stolid as timber,
And star on star chimes over them, while below
The waters that give life roar querulous.

Blue fumes from the sleeping flowers,
Ripening the kernels, waking the thirst to grow,
Things germinate, fall to fecund, damp soil.
The dark eyes of hirsute peasants burn
Among girls swarthy and buxom.
The angel of the forest bends to lure us
Among warm moss.

The zodiac, swaddled in the sky's parchment
Appears to us in crucifixes nightly
And the dreams of our faith, a burning poppy…

Dead stars still glitter in our eyes, their light
Shines on the red cockerel, summoning a pale blue moon.
This is beauty, the primal thunder, a storm…

So religions and societies are born
In some epic evening, the sky the blue

Banner of life tumultuous, I glorify!

The First Chapter of the Bible

When the stone still sang and the serpent had wings
And Eve dressed in a fig leaf,
The wind blew more wild and drunken,
The sea beneath the stars shone silver.

When Eve tore the moon from an apple tree,
And the lions rebelled in paradise,
When Adam's sons scattered through the world,
Rearing the towns and palaces for Eve.

Nuptial

For Olechka

Listen as the nuptial tambourine beats
And the maples bow like peacocks,
The curved moon plaits
Itself in your hair, my beloved.

Why has the violin fallen to a whisper,
And why does your hand tremble?
The night's silver covers all like moss,
The moon is shoeing a horse.

The Wedding Night

The night is on fire with bird song.
Who will lay out our bed, beloved?
Look at the moon in the window glittering
In the window a chalice of magic above.

We two, a cruciform of love and moss,
Plaited together by crazy happiness.
The morning trembles with a hundred moons,
Our passionate fecund dreams.

Hops

Girl, redolent of vernal hops,
You twine around me,
Woodpeckers coo to us from dreaming moss,
Where leaves flutter in hundreds of forests.

Spring's nuptial blossom respires
And each night is a rich poison,
With your palms smooth as hops
And our secret, unfathomable happiness.

Two Hearts

In the evening, in the horizon, in song
We go embracing, ahead.
Like a tile from a roof the wind tears
Stars from the sky.

And leaving the throng we fold away
Into the recess of night.
Let two hearts as doves sing
At the pitch of yearning.

Hooves

Spring comes on one hundred wagons,
Violin bows tauten their bowstrings
Among the finely sifted spring rains.
The deacon lights a candle.

Though we are not ready to leave
When the double bass barely reaches us,
Let it be the moon, my love,
With which the blacksmith shoes our horse.

Periwinkle Sincerity

Love me mundanely and simply,
As all girls love,
When you cross the white bridge, a star,
Catches in your hair.

Only those who kiss for the first time
Can kiss so ardently,
In your fledgling words' tremor I sense
A periwinkle's sincerity.

A Little Hymn

The arrow intends to fly,
The string is tuned to play,
The crimson stars are coins
Laid in the evening's purse

The heart? Just intoxicate
Shake and love it.
The wind a hundredfold I glorify,
And spring I praise multiply.

Market

My brother was the tailor of boyish dreams,
Stitching the sky to the earth,
Headscarves blaze on the shopkeepers' pates
Multi-coloured crests, carpenters

Sing, drums beat
And I'll reveal the secret…
They are selling the sun
At Horlitsi Market.

Cuckoo

Oh the cuckoo calls again
Perhaps that's the hundredth one?
In my youthful rambling of twenty springs
I have measured time with songs.

Dew silvers raspberries,
A lad prays to the spring,
The minutes fly by with cuckoos
Boys are painted with dream.

The Home Beyond the Stars

The hymn of plants electric sings of growth's freedom
And the heart, as if it were on its seventh glass,
Is unspeakably drunk. I leave, already a chance guest,
Who will pray to other stars, for other mornings yearn.

The swollen buds plump into the sap, sticky foam
Of bloom like a star clasped to a plant in a kiss,
Night filters spring's magic through violet glass,
Handfuls of fragrance in petalled chalices borne.

Vegetable night and green stifled with ecstasy,
Blissful bush tangle, roots, fingers and leaves
Seed explodes, moon rolls around earth its horn,
Till day expires in the last serpentine flitter

And lush roots fibrous weave through skulls, life
Drills crudely into the tangles of death.
Oak grapples with oak, two angry gods strike
And disperse into foam, stubbornly interwoven.

The circles of light wheel unbroken as day
Grinds night into the annunciation of dawn.
Drink seven glasses of happiness, let the heart fly!
Poetry seething and wise as greenery!

I have lived only for a brief moment, not knowing
If I will live more. So let me study the drunkenness
Of plants, the growth and rage of sap!
Maybe my home is elsewhere, beyond the stars
While I am here I feel instinctively

To sing is to exist
While water seethes beneath the carapace of soil
And the edge of the sky is a violet wall of mist,
I walk through the valley to the sun's lyre as it rises,
Praising growth, superhuman, vegetable tempest.

Science

Learn your craft from carpenters,
Learn to carve the words.
As spring sails lyrically past
It will again be the summer of the axe.

I burn with the axe's prayer,
Bearing verses from silver,
The migrating song of words
Beneath the blue moss clouds.

To the Depths

I carved a poem from silver,
A poem like a fir,
Spring stopped and turned pale,
A shocked girl.

Sing axe, and crazy carpenters
Hew out a song again,
In depths where I jag the singing blade
Into the roots of words.

Daily Bread

In the depth, the essence, the root of things, the womb
The core of words and the core of the sun!
In the squall of ecstasy when the slenderest
Thing tears the veil of consciousness
Deep from us, a dead skin. The lily softens in dreams,

The white furls of its skirt fade,
To a cylinder robed in gold.
The earth is riveted with fire, the sun
Cleft in two by the horizon,
Azure perspectives mingle,
In the wind's curved membrane.
Drowsy people pass like dreams,
Oscillating on the rope of sunstruck mornings.
Language flexes
         Drunkenly,
In anguished joy,
A node of light distorting
On a razor.
I tear into jealous death
By songs
As the depths of the earth,
    The depths of the densest words,
Are torn ardently
    By exaltation,
    By night and day.

The Sign of the Oak

Beyond the dam of three days and three night, where the
                                                    numbed vortex
Of unplumbed green was half conscious, endless…
Fettered to tree stumps, the harnessed winds, the god of
                                                    terror,
Centuries old and cunning, has an utterly new face.
Creepers, moist earthly lightning, snake through dead trees,
Slippery with dew milky and chill.

Night banally erodes outlines into mere blemishes;
Only the oak squats amidst its green currencies.
The star balances on its ray, as on a cane above the ravine
Where the badger conceals its taciturn malice,
The marsh ceremonially incenses the air with spores golden
As night, a black boar, tusked with moon, a pelt vegetable
                                                    and coarse.

The incapacity of countless forms, the wealth ordained for
                                                    the dark,
Above wilderness of sky, human fear and ecstasy, the dead
                                                    light,
Only the oak proud and leonine, a stout monarch,
Guides the sun to this vain world, a sceptre lording it.

Orchard

A biological verse in two cases

1

Words vibrate like bees in the rain,
Conversations are broken when they've barely begun,
Thoughts ignite and are swiftly hidden,
The fleeting gaze bright, deft as a butterfly wing.

The room flowers into an orchard for us,
We plait together with our coiled leaves,
I grow my root in you and dew burns
Silver in our incandescent dreams.

2

We two, are two dense bushes interwoven,
Our smile, the soft flash of a butterfly wing,
Thoughts penetrate like bees in the rain,
Buzz, pinned fast to the sharpest thorn.

Songs like berries bloom daily,
In the orchard where we thrive,
Embraced by leaves so closely,
And the vegetable god of love

Grows root deep, pure and primal.

Tavern Enchantments

The smoking candle and notched knife,
The red queen from a deck of cards,
Reality mixed with a winged dream, all
Is unreal, just night and a witch's spell.

Lips tremble on the rim of a glass,
My heart brims with gloom.
Innkeeper! I'll give you one hundred ducats,
Just sell me the moon!

Haymaking

The mower sticks the sun in his belt,
A pointed bar,
The day opens deeper and wider, the way
He rolls his sleeves up more.

The words of the singing hay balers
Are themselves baled into verses,
Their inspiring labours conclude
With sweat dabbed from a forehead.

A Fig of a Verse

The night, already warm with drunken flowers,
Fades into a mist of bird cherry blooms
Where letters, like the stars, shine still
In the open book laid on the table.

Leaves sprout and engulf it all, so lush
That I and the chair are already a bush,
Reading the bird cherry's vast book, lost
In the vegetable wisdom of eternal forests.

The Guelder Rose

The guelder rose bows down,
The red word grows like a berry,
Pray to the aspiring spring,
Carve its song in stone.

The sunray is an arrow,
Piercing the word, shearing through rock,
But only the guelder rose blooms
Every year with leaves, its songs.

Skiers

Shallow silver pools lay
On foothill, mountain and forest,
Ahead, on the hop, sideways,
Straightforward and athwart.

Cold water of mountain wind,
Washes our lungs
The vigour of the frost, so youthful,
Tempers our hands to steel.

Searing strength of frost crackle,
Sharpens breath like a blade,
Bare white waves above
Fleet from our eyes as we vault.

Unstoppable, we float
In unbroken pursuit,
Heart pounds its mallet,
Heart beats its bell,
We pierce the horizon,
The red sun cartwheeling,

In a bonny race,
We cleave heaven's hemisphere, descending dementedly
Through branches, jagging blue sky
And shaggy pine tree.
We set the world afire with the wind's torch;
Let the methyl of our wrath blaze.
We bob repeatedly up slopes, left and right,
Greeting the night.

On the wings of our waxed skis drive away
Pain from our hearts utterly
Heart pounds like a mallet
Heart beats like a bell.

A harsh happiness found
If only for a moment
Among the high rocks,
And bellowed at the eagles,
Weaving our way randomly
Towards our goal, with a cry
Of victory we flow
Over life's snow.

Winter

Tailors stitch new pelts for the foxes,
Winds funnel threats into a storm,
O lord, in this crazed blizzard, keep
Human and animal nests from harm.

In a hundred mills the winter
Grinds wheat to snow, blue silver,
Night sparkles to welcome the storm,
Burying the village in heaven.

Sunset

Curled clouds above the meadow,
Sheep pastured by the moon,
Girls, like the grass, grow,
Delighting lads and men.

Bulls pierce the sun with their horns,
Till the blood flows from him,
The field turns crimson,
This sunset, a wound steaming.

Antonych Grows

Antonych grows and the grass grows,
And the alders turn deeper green.
Oh just lean, lean closer to them,
You'll hear the most secret of all words.

Do not trouble with April showers, spring!
Who sprinkles you with crystalline leaves,
Who emptied the glass jug of the sky?
Do you want to catch the rain in a sieve?

The strangest of all forest languages;
Someone loads night's rifle with stars,
Cuckoos perched on alders peck the moon.
Antonych grows and the grass grows

Cherries

Antonych used to feed on cherries and was a beetle,
The same cherries of which Shevchenko sang.
My country, stellar, proud and biblical,
Flowering fatherland of cherry and nightingale!

Where there are evenings of gospel clarity,
Where white villages are razed with sunlight at dawn,
Cherries, heart lifting, bloom, curled and drunkenly,
And with Shevchenko's hops sluice song again.

Myth

As if in some pre-Aryan book,
Horse shoes, boats and arrows,
Armour glittering in the woods.
The murmur of Sanskrit words.

Blonde and slender, the tribesmen come,
Accustomed to ships and horses.
Above the auspicious stars burn,
A flight of sabres cruciform.

The Emissaries of Night

The sun docks at the oak, rearing
Seven red oars in valediction,
Slender poplars sustain the sky
Through my window.
I am silent before night's emissaries.
Will you come? they ask,
To where your brother tends the stars,
An idol among vineyards of cloud,

And gardens where dresses float,
As the kalyna turns pale at night,
The door of music opening
On recesses of light?
You cast your eyes on its berries,
Their rich azure in the darkness,
As if you were the first scribe
Writing the laws of harmony

In a cuneiform script.
Above you the light
Burns its silvered tallow
In cauldrons of cold stars,
The stalks snake, green candles
Lighting your way to Hades.
Your horse is a black flame,
The captive gale,

The milk spray of its mane
Glows against the darkness,
Its legs beat like oars
To the call of distant roads.
Its nostrils flare.

Our heart is torn in two,
Eternally. Our brains
Rest delicately as flowers,

In the vase of the skull.

The Wind of Centuries

The wind blows from centuries,
Soaring, free and indomitable,
Teaching us freedom and yearning
For something unknown and untamed.

It repeats to us the same thing,
Lost and broken, vainly,
That life cannot be stopped,
Is not a dormitory.

Village

The sun sticks fast between two maples,
Wind raises dust from a ditch,
The field's green vortex
Swirls round the sun.

The river is a sash, the forest a stripe,
Grass rears into a flood,
The plough repeats its requiem
Where war once trod.

Roofs

Village swathed in alder and hazel,
With its roofs of red tile,
You wrap, as in a skirt, in the blue sky
As you wrap youth in mystery.

Remember the guelder-rosed riverbank,
Shepherds watering the sun in the well?
Write a story of fragrant evenings,
Meditating alders, the roofs' crimson belt.

Circle

I return among alders and fish,
To where there is mint, ivy, walls of flowers,
Again I kiss the black furrows,
Falling on my knees before the sun.

Oh, it bows over me, burning
As a mother bows over her son,
Again the earth drinks its fill of me
As flowers kiss dew crazily.

The black furrows and blue stream
Hang like a skirt on the clouds' body.
Here, among curled grass, I was born
Beneath the alders and the sun.

Country of Annunciation

Blizzard green, green flame,
Flowers' curves, nightingales' warbling.
The wedding table, as yet uncovered,
And bees dark, so dark, and lime trees praying.

In a song of camomile a snail winds its way,
The morning, a basket with a bird inside,
The sweep of sunlight…
Thoughts are not thoughts, sadness is not sadness,
But a tragic tumour on this country.

Dragons of sun and moon rear the Galician Star…
Pale villages flame against the greenness,
The pale dust,
Above the road where Shevchenko comes,
A fire, a man, a storm,
And peers
Into the distance of centuries.

Amidst the flames
A princess awakens.

Let them brand the earth before our eyes, its black pit
                                                mouth,
Where day is not day and night is not night
And we are bereft of psalms.

Oh earth, oh soil of my fathers, cursed immutably
Oh country
Of annunciation!

Two Chapters from the Liturgy of Love

1

Your smile is tranquil as a flower,
For your essence is open and clear
To this empty world where you bloom
And burn with beauty to live more,

More and broader and higher still!
Oh send more light! And more sun send!
No, we still have not taken from life all
That is needful in the end.

Let only our sacramental lips be,
Green fills the world's desert
Just that vital fragment of joy
Torn ardently from fate.

2

Your smile has a flower's quietness,
Sister of light, the more you shine!
Protect us from this boundless,
Heedless world, blossom of mine!

When our brother, the evening, bears us
Sheaves of stars, lilies of the valley,
It is no sin, but a song divine
Burns in my heart with longing.

Plainsong sings our hearts, you walk
Perfect as a brief story,
So it was, and always will be,
Love is kind and revelatory.

To a Proud Plant, that is, to Myself

Broad shouldered tree stumps. Worms and June,
The silver of extinguished stars
Powders onto oak leaves. The depths
Of subterranean rivers. Primal plants tremble.

The cloudlet a kerchief upon heaven's face.
The worm sings the anthem of corruption.
The arc in early morning sky, a solar eyebrow.
Fragmented sunrays, slender silver grass stalks.

The green dome of arrow tree-topped oak,
Raised from the niches of night.
Dawn's fire hunting worms and corruption,
God stubbornly infusing earth with fresh sap.

Electric of the green earth he fires into plants
Like live and copper wire, but you
Are the proudest of them and yet sing,
Though sometime like a stump you will be
Defeated of the body and will roll over
The earth borne on shoulders blue.

Rotation

So the multilevel sounds of the city run through the alley.
Height after height, falling on another like notes in a chord.
The diurnal street clamour, where yellow walls are a levee,
Seethes between banks in garlands of oak shadow.

The day compels, with its light, a glass of gold tea,
Purged azure and acoustic cloud.
People walk the sepia streets, their eyes gleaming,
Though they conceal sorrow within, a bitter seed.

Churches, confectioneries, wagon halts, travel
Through the body and spirit and stars fall
To coins in a pocket beyond happiness, some other goal,
Despair probes the wound that is our soul.

From over the wall we hear jazz, the dance of lanterns
And gas canisters, a choir of colours and oboes
In the yellow breasts of vast stadiums,
The deafening sigh of the crowd, its human storms.

A ceiling of smoke levitates up my legs, the compliant birds
                                                                                                         fly,
The sun, a spider casts its arc of light askance on the wall,
The spider's web's crimson antennae crucify
Dead insects, the sounds they catch and kill.

Plants are artists, tulips attentive to form,
Fall to their knees and beautifully, colourfully perish,
In accord with scientific formulae, unknown
Dental probes of days and towns all excavate us.

Trembling nerves of wire, the warm white sheet
Is a star in an envelope with some words and dog rose petals,
As withered leaves, the dreams of dentists twist
Above cavities and turgid melodies of dental drills.

Of Cities and Muses

Amid oak leaves, merchants' scales and gypsies,
Daily clamour and eternal nightly stars,
Life is the most difficult of arts. A reprimand
For each wasted day. Night waits, the harsh judge,

And sweet-voiced lips betray. Perhaps no memory
Will remain of anguish ploughing our forehead.
The overcoat, a wing penduluming from the shoulder,
The wind wafting its wings over our home,

Coils of smoke lasso the city with the sky.

Heroes, homosexuals and poets really
Pure as flowers and a speckle on the bed sheet,
Day and night boys shamefully taste their sweetness,
Among the jokes of cheats and dark pits of sorrow.

Somewhere the hurdy-gurdy cries, light splays
Stripes across faces like peacock feathers,
And human fate is cheap paper that sways
In a parrot's curved beak:
Love
Journeys
Separation
Glory
Success.

Twenty farthings can buy happiness,
A day of woven and unravelling smiles,
Parrot song and sun in gold communion.

Unexpected encounter. Orchestras play in the parks.
Decent families with lots of kids come,
The malicious wind that wrenches us with despair inspiredly
Has already died. Bunches of cards and cloud flight.

The winged shadow of fate. A fragile reed and propitiatory
                                                                                        flowers.
We capture the stream of inspiration in numbers,
Weird marvel,
How we dress, the smallest matters in cramped and blunt
                                                                                        truth,
Though only the wisdom
Of ecstasy is infallible.

War Drum

So the rotund sun is the tambourine of morning,
Rousing the soldiers to march and war drums
Beat around the barracks, while spring
Is a bird warbling along
The cells of grey corridors as day sketches its path
On the map of heaven, the stars
Expire, like the eyes of fatigued lovers.
The maples are a rainstorm of colour,
Spring
Ignites sunrise, taking wing,
Drunk with life,
And the wind plays
In the maples
As if they were the brass trumpets of dawn.
Girls faint into a stranger's arms,
With bird-like cries.
Drowsy eyes open, hearing
The bang of the soldiers' war drum,
The war drum of spring, heard on buses,
Its song alarming the heart as it sounds,
The drum of death.
The words of young lovers,
Words like money, expunged of passion,
Grow dumb.

But this seething life
Can never be fettered, spring
Utters its command
To delight uplifting
Unrestrained triumph, error strewn
The black cubes of barracks stand
By drumming with boots, parade ground

And morning beats upon
The tambourine of sun.

Ballad of the Alleyway

Where night wrings its blue hands to call
For salvation in vain,
Where drunks and shadows wobble,
The streetlight is lame,

Is a fading lily, an azure flower
In a world unreal.
Where mice guide shoemakers
To the drunk moon, bells

And stars ring in the tavern, as shysters
And chimney sweeps sing
Hymns over glasses brimming,
Praising night and sin.

She's a mean bitch, The Lady of Sorrows,
Stooping to bank breakers,
Her face a sponge lined with furrows,
Fake cards in her fingers,

The favourites of this nightly trade lean
On their elbows in thought,
Float on a linen of smoke and murmurs,
Stars in a violin case chat.

In a nest of illusion, ranting, scandals
Parrots tell fortunes
To trembling birds, by sobbing candles,
Hammering words into the table.

The cutthroat cries for nothing and believes
Only in horilka, his God
And, like a spider, forgotten song weaves
Into his gorge, torn into bits.

Again the chimney sweeps praise life,
With a muttered hymn
Like a banner
But who slammed the tankard down?

Glasses, like birds, fly away
Over the table, under the ceiling
The wafting of each glass wing
Sets chimes playing
Beneath the blue shrubbery of smoke
That roofs the inn.

The last star faded,
As the moon had to fade,
And, in the broken shell of skull,
The choir of shysters and sweeps
Will murmur and chat at least
Till morning breaks.

The Ballad of Azure Death

Buildings spectral at dusk, boxed courtyards,
Thicketed gloom with narrow, dank steps,
Nocturnal abysses that no one has yet measured
And the sorrow of dark gates and reek of mould.

A crumpled and speckled scrap of paper
Briefly inscribed: "no one is guilty,
Seek no criminal!" The moon steps soundless
As a cat over the roofs. A moth flutters.

Bouquets of steam ooze from open pipes,
Azure blood from bloated veins.
The spectral solo of a clarinet's grief
Raves dementedly from behind the wardrobe.

Falls asleep in fear. The soul burns azure,
Crazed whispers cradle two hearts above
The psyche; night's deranged vortex!
Gas flowers through torn rugs of silence.

The bed, boat of love and weariness,
Where a moonlit mouse sits, bob tailed
And cynical … body with body, plaited
For the last time twist in sweet pain unsated,

The angel of gas leans above them
Crowned with an azure flame,
Like myrrh, lilies cast into ecstasy,
Each soul burns with alcohol

In fire's transparency.

Doomsday Cometh

The cloud of ravens, dark linen
Settles on the rucked roof, moon
Waves its blue hands, a prophet
Cursing the city,

For all sins and trespasses
For vanity, treachery depravity
For all the crimes this nest
Of scorn and scallywags brims with.

So ne'er-do-wells and Harpagons
Sing psalms atoning,
Calibans clang bells and Hetaeras
Neigh like mares.

Loathsome, shameful and dead
Luoisas rise from their beds
And Sardanapalus's proud victims
Sharpen their red tongues.

As twelve arrows fire from the sky,
Twelve winds descend
Earth's ravine maw opens, sun's
Circle is sheared to bits.

Distant subterranean thunder, bells
Clang against walls, city into abyss
Tumbles beneath the racket
Of wings and megaphones. That's it.

A Concert from Mercury

Night lowers its lid on the ant's nest of the town,
Bitter almonds of dream grow among valleys of
                                        forgetfulness,
Stars, leaf shoals spin above the human
Whirlpool, now dreaming wealth and agonies,

Antennae sprout strong on roofs, a herb that sings in the
                                                      wind,
As lovers interweave, hop vines in summer,
Rooms red lobsters of street light slither around,
The body cools in dreams, where the soul dies, fungus daubs
                                                        it silver.

My russet lover lays in her warm bed, with a star in her case
Old feathers, wet roses and book worms. On a radio station
The announcer picks up the moon's disc and plays
Visible music on night's cold gramophone.

Dead Cars

Fragments of broken stars, they sleep in the machine
                                              cemetery,
The dead cars and the red flower of rust measure minutes,
And years ripened in copper and only the unknowable solar
                                                      glitter
Sways over them, an eternal truth also imperceptible to us,
Like the blue fragrance of petrol.
Sometimes the dead harry us,
Like jackals in dreams
And the wares of their desires and thirst and needs are
                                                      displayed
As at a bazaar,
And dead torsos in the blue dark of night,
Lay in the sinful beds of whores and twisters,
Whose inauspicious stars blur.
As we dig the bones of lizards from under the rocks of
                                                    forgotten eras,
So, one day someone will dig our metal bones from here.
Girls with a nameless flower,
Hands engendering bread and green rue,
And new cities with squares hung where now is azure sky
                                                      will come,
Heat romping like lions in them.

We will be restless shadows, unquiet ghosts,
From under city squares, from under grass!

Oh Metropolis,

Between your red walls the weightless
Souls of cars drift!

The Last Trumpet

The hundred-storeyed stone towers sleep, fatigued creatures,
Geographers chalk stars on the map of the heavens,
Rain feathers through a street lamp's blonde radiance
Like sand, and the moon curls its gold cat on my divan.

Dead fish rust in basins among coal and roses, black,
The merchants, the naked girls, prisoners and poets,
The orchestra of policemen plays a melancholy tune
On pipe and French horn.
The nondescript god tots up stars, souls and coins.

They live below the town, as in a story, the whales, dolphins
                                                      and Tritons
In water viscous and black as tar, in cellars of fear,
With the fern's curled nightmare

Griffins, drowned comets and bells.
Oh, thicket of stone,
When will the deluge wash you clean?

A Poem about the Breezes

The glassy eyes of stones
And the foreheads of balconies above them,
Where swarms of colours dance,
The radiance of paint and tones…

O city, city, city,
With your gigantic iron and concrete palisades
O city, city, city,
Blue haze of sky where your profile fades,

With the diamond pupils of the breeze.

The glassy eyes of stones,
Above them reliefs and facades,
The mutating dance of adverts, a caress
Alluring and poisonous.

O city, city, city,
With your gigantic iron and concrete palisades
O city, city, city,
Your reliefs denting the breeze.

To stare into your glass transparencies
Oh vertical enchanted lakes:
Do silver fish bask here,
Fashioned from the moon's lustre?

. . . .

It is so good to look into your unblemished

    windows

Oh grief slashed by the place where the breeze

   plays

In a rain of reflexes mushrooms of story

   sprout

Those tiny, inane chocolate Melusinas…

. . . .

A thousand impassioned eyes

Shiver over your skin

And your laughter is the rose

Glare of streetlights

A thousand times your fist is a kiss

Entice

Among the glitter of deluges

Alluring darkness.

In georgette, silk and brocade

Crepe de chine

Gathered coils of flowers

perpetual wooden smiles

of manikins

squares, rectangles, rhomboids,

rhombuses.

The glassy eyes of stones,
Reliefs, friezes and facades,
The pale moon cauldron,
The street lights commune.

O city, city, city,
With your gigantic iron and concrete palisades,
O city, city, city,
Cry with the quadratic breeze.

The stone's glassy eyes,
Boudoirs whispering with dream,
Nocturnal shadows come
On squares, parks, pavements,
Oh city, do not fear

Her conclusion,

O city, the breeze slams shutters against a window

Waving you a brisk cheerio.

Night

Mixture of clouds with stars as with rye,
Night hoists it on its back and walks,
A golden dough is kneaded
In the moon's round trough.

Drunk girls roll like thunder
As Taurus bellows,
Fecund earth, and water quick
With ripples of music.

Green Faith

Green God of animals and plants,
Teach me the faith intoxicating,
The religion of nocturnal spring,
When primal life seethes, changing
All that is unchangeable.
(The religion of nights that boil,
Thundering green cloud vegetable).

Green God of storms and growth,
Reduce to ash my bones
That they may sprout, and so seethe
Green body of plants drunken.

Who are you bowing your coiled head
Fire or bird, storm or god?

Musica Noctis

Night Music

The moon, a pallid torch kindled in heaven,
The nocturnal darkness lit with stars.
Let the heart, sick with loneliness, find solace
Under the gaze of your thousands of worlds.

In the heart, swathed in the scarves of quiet peace,
Each tone sounds gentle and harmonious.
Distance echoes with barely audible harps,
The wind tunes night with God's tuning fork.

A matured summer bridled with spring, beautiful,
Its ripe abundance has bloomed in your soul.
Though slightly darker, grey tones brush the horizon,
The distance where the sun's gold cupola sets.

The warm summer night bears the scent
Of many flowers unto the mountain summits.
Let us listen to the vast concert of twilight,
When God's hands brush the piano of the world.

Amen

The concert finished,
Only the echo, a deception
Lingers, the end of all things,
Death, secret and unknown.

Joy and sorrow
Fleet like a bad dream
Already God lays me
In a case like a violin.

The end of all song,
The string plays no more
But let the heart sing
These words unspoken.

You must change your heart
So that it may sing,
Not needing much to be happy.
Just harmony.
    Amen.

De Morte IV

I am calm as silence on water,
I have enough, enough power
Not to fear even when
Something bat-like stares into my eyes.

When its wings waft overhead,
And my eyes sting, immersed in blood,
That will be the mute language
Of one sole word, death.

Even its spectral darkness
Cannot unstring my spirit.
Lord, let me stubborn, withstand
The breakers and not bend.

Lord let me in the contest
Stand, a rock against the horde
So that my death will be the last
Harmonising chord.

Idolatrous Nights

The refraction of the moon repeats itself in the clouds, a
                                                                 song,
Cloud on cloud forming a silver wall, below which the foxes
                                                                 bark.
Leaves dangle from the stars in oblique ropes,
The mushrooms chime their plates of rust colour,

In the forest choir,
The leaves of the oak form
A lush foam, a surf, that booms and trumpets
The unwritten law of night.
Wolves bring their sacrifice of blood and flesh,
Wiping their muzzles on musical flax.
Night of predatory law and dark magic. In the marsh things
                                                                 knead
A dull red dough of mud. Owls harmonise treason.

A star wrinkles its eyebrow at the moon,
Flower sticks to flower,
In a dew thick as paste,
The oily greenery
Becomes this coarse fabric of darkness.
The angles of roots are coiled music, plaiting
The melodies that foam within.
This is the heart of the forest,
The horizon's secret,
Where storms exhaust themselves and lightning
Is a razor whipped across a razor,
Each broken human dream.
Its wings sweep across the earth, adorning roofs
With wreathes for the marriage of fire.
Terror, a subterranean child that cries each night

In that place where beyond knowledge of feeling or ruin
The incomprehensible, ancient speech surrounds us.
The river. Spring grinds its ice.

In Conclusion

Who needs your words?
They who weigh bread and salt,
They who calculate interest?
They who in some sleepless night
Print a rebellious decree?
They who burn with fever
And ferocious hunger?
They who tear down prison walls
Or those who guard the jails?

Also from Kalyna Language Press

The August Rain is PEN award winning poet and translator Stephen Komarnyckyj's first collection of original poetry. *This is a book through which memory and its voices lap like waves. Whether it be in his own luminous writing, or through his translations and versions of others, Komarnyckyj communicates a quiet fire that is often 'stringent as redemption'.*
Sean Street, Poet and BBC Broadcaster.
Drawing force both from an English visionary tradition that leads right back to Caedmon and the fevered restlessness of some Slavic poetries, Stephen Komarnyckyj's is a serious poetry of life's elemental mysteries and sorrows.
Vivek Narayanan, Poet.

My father, with his trousers rolled up to his knee,
Stood in the beck, in peat-stained water
That was the gold orange of a delicate tea,
Though curious frills of lace and snow
Bloomed over the stones nearby
And his feet were either bronze or ivory.

From *Tickling*